IMAGES
of America

LOGAN COUNTY

On September 28, 1928, the local newspaper, the *Logan Banner*, reported that a dedication of the World War I doughboy soldier statue was held on the Logan County Courthouse grounds in Logan, West Virginia. A well-attended event, several politicians spoke from the courthouse steps. Years later, after the construction of a new courthouse, the statue was relocated to Midelburg Island near the Logan High School campus. (Courtesy of the author's collection.)

ON THE COVER: In 1952, there were numerous activities planned in the city of Logan to celebrate the 100th anniversary of its founding. Mayor Litz "Cuz" McGuire (in top hat) is shown on horseback on Jefferson Street during the centennial celebration parade. The centennial celebration was held September 10–13, 1952. (Courtesy of the author's collection.)

IMAGES
of America

LOGAN COUNTY

F. Keith Davis

ARCADIA
PUBLISHING

Copyright © 2011 by F. Keith Davis
ISBN 978-1-5316-5473-3

Published by Arcadia Publishing
Charleston, South Carolina

Library of Congress Control Number: 2010942070

For all general information, please contact Arcadia Publishing:
Telephone 843-853-2070
Fax 843-853-0044
E-mail sales@arcadiapublishing.com
For customer service and orders:
Toll-Free 1-888-313-2665

Visit us on the Internet at www.arcadiapublishing.com

*To Logan County: May this bring about the fondest of memories.
And to Cheryl Fortune Davis: Thank you for your
encouragement and invaluable assistance.*

CONTENTS

ACKNOWLEDGMENTS

This book represents my humble attempt at bringing interesting photographs and accurate historical information together to authentically tell in broad strokes the story of Logan County. Although it would easily take dozens of volumes to give a more complete account of this area, I hope this project will be accepted as a starting point for those interested in learning more about this region's rich history, complex culture, and proud people.

I would like to express my sincere gratitude to historians from the past whose documented words provided a wealth of information invaluable to me in my research, including Coleman A. Hatfield, Coleman C. Hatfield, G.T. Swain, Robert Y. Spence, L.E. Thompson, John Ferrell, E.H. Howerton, Claude Ellis, G.W. Raike, Grady Yeager, Merrill Atkinson, Bruce Harris, and Wib Whited.

I am also grateful for the resources available from local newspaper publications, including the *Logan County Banner* (which later became the *Logan Banner*), *Logan Democrat*, *Logan News*, *Fayette Journal*, *Huntington Dispatch*, and the *Charleston Gazette*, as well as the West Virginia Archives.

This book would not have been possible without the accessibility of these prior works: *History of Logan County, WV* by G.T. Swain (2010); *Centennial Program, City of Logan, West Virginia, 1852–1952*; *The Tale of the Devil: The Biography of Anderson "Devil Anse" Hatfield* by Dr. Coleman C. Hatfield and Robert Y. Spence (2008); *Land of the Guyandot: A History of Logan County* by Robert Y. Spence (1976); *West Virginia Tough Boys* by F. Keith Davis (2003); *West Virginia Disasters: Mountain State Tragedies That Have Changed Our Lives* compiled by CNHI Newspapers of West Virginia (2005); and *The Feuding Hatfields & McCoys* by Dr. Coleman C. Hatfield and F. Keith Davis (2008).

Lastly, it is also important to acknowledge Joe Hensley, Drew Martin, Ken Scaggs, Sherri Scaggs Smith, Bob Barker, Jack Cyfers, Raamie Barker, Richard Osborne, Tim and Susie Hiroskey, Michael Taylor, James Fortune, Charles T. Murphy, and everyone who submitted photographs to me or provided historical information through the years; and I especially want to thank Debrina Williams and the Logan County Chamber of Commerce for their support and encouragement.

Unless otherwise noted, all images appear courtesy of the author.

INTRODUCTION

It was a scenic and unique place. And although picturesque, it was also an unforgiving and demanding region that required equally unique and tenacious people to possess it. Logan County, nestled in the cradle of the beautiful Appalachian Mountains in southern West Virginia, has a distinctive and vibrant history that dates back to the first recorded inhabitants who spoke in the Algonquin tongue.

In 1774, after the passing of beloved Chief Cornstalk, Princess Aracoma, the chief's daughter, led her people to the territory and settled at the island. From the beginning, the tribe exhibited affection for the Guyan Valley and an appreciation for the peaceful seclusion and protection found amongst the local mountain range.

With daring and grit and from meager beginnings, others began to arrive in the Guyan basin and carve out an existence from the Appalachian wilderness, including early colonists and European travelers. It was also a time when a young nation celebrated its independence from Great Britain, and families were looking for new adventures. Soon a steady stream of pioneers—some traveling by flatboat or raft, others by horseback or covered wagon—began to arrive in the valley.

By 1824, Logan County was formed and named in honor of Chief Logan, head of the Mingo tribe.

In the late 1870s, just a few years after Gen. Robert E. Lee surrendered at Appomattox Courthouse, many people in Logan still harbored deep scars from the Civil War, and tensions ran high. It was at this time that the county became known as the home of the feuding Hatfields—a land cursed as the locale of America's most violent family vendetta. Although gunshots were silenced around 1891, the region is still haunted by the drama of the two warring families.

This period was also marked by the development of the timber and coal industries and the arrival of the Chesapeake & Ohio Railroad (C&O). Coal companies began purchasing tracts of land, hiring personnel, and building communities.

It has long been said that, in Logan County, coal is king. However, over the decades, the difficult and dangerous working conditions of a deep mine and the meager wages and lack of respect shown by coal operators have worn heavily on the county's coal workers.

According to the West Virginia Archives, by 1919, the largest nonunionized coal region in the eastern United States consisted of Logan and Mingo Counties. It was at this time that the United Mine Workers of America (UMWA) made southwestern West Virginia its highest priority. Meanwhile, the Logan Coal Operators Association hired Sheriff Don Chafin and paid for an expanded deputy force to keep union organizers away, violently confronting, harassing, or even arresting those participating in labor gatherings.

Labor tensions came to a bloody climax during the Battle of Blair Mountain, the largest armed labor conflict in US history. On August 24, 1921, approximately 5,000 protesting miners began to march from Kanawha County, each wearing red bandanas (thus nicknamed "rednecks"). Meanwhile, from his command post in Logan, Sheriff Chafin mobilized an opposing militia consisting of well-armed deputies, merchants, state police, and mine guards.

At the request of West Virginia governor Ephraim Morgan, Pres. Warren G. Harding became directly involved. When faced with possible charges of treason, many miners and UMWA leaders turned back. However, others marched on from the community of Sharples, and a battle soon resulted at Blair Mountain. By September 1, President Harding sent federal troops to the area. Confronted with the possibility of fighting against US troops, most of the remaining miners surrendered, although some continued until September 4. During the fighting, at least a dozen miners as well as four men from Chafin's army were killed.

After the conflict ended, Governor Morgan used National Guard troops to discourage miners from taking up arms again. Nevertheless, the UMWA gained a foothold in southern West Virginia, and working conditions improved over the coming years.

Throughout the decades, the strength and courage of Logan County's people have been tested and retested. It would seem the region has endured more than its share of devastating flash floods, rock falls, mine disasters, train derailments, and other calamities. For example, 18 miners working at Holden Mine No. 22 perished as a slate fall and fire trapped them in the mine on March 8, 1960. In more recent years, on January 19, 2006, two miners paid the ultimate cost of mining, losing their lives at Aracoma Alma Mine in Melville.

One of the largest disasters in US history took place at Buffalo Creek in Logan County on February 26, 1972. A 30-foot wall of water, sludge, and debris came roaring through Buffalo Creek Hollow after a Pittston Coal Company slurry impoundment dam burst. Within minutes, 125 miners were dead, 1,100 were injured, and 4,000 Logan County residents were left homeless. Seven miners were never found. Property damage exceeded $50 million.

Even in the face of these dark challenges, the people of Logan County have remained resilient. It would seem that overcoming adversity and obstacles, while working hard and accomplishing worthy goals, has become a way of life for those who call this region home; and in a way, it is these very adversities—and the responses to these challenges—that have shaped the land and guided the course of its future.

Those who have moved away seem to always harbor a deep love for their homeland as well as a strong desire to return; and visitors to the area describe its people as the "friendliest folks in America." Residents of Logan County have worked hard and been rewarded for their accomplishments. They have built successful business enterprises, formed lasting friendships, and raised happy, productive families. Many have lived the American Dream in these hills, carving out existences that have brought about personal fulfillment while hoping to pass on a bright future to their children and grandchildren.

Logan still has much to offer, including an intriguing landscape and an environment that has nurtured an equally intriguing people. As from the beginning, Logan County is full of opportunity, yet it still requires a tenacious people willing to possess it.

One

COMMUNITY AND PEOPLE

Carter's Studio, a local photography business, took this snapshot of Logan from the Dingess Street intersection. The photographer was looking eastward down Stratton Street, and the view depicts the county seat at a time when the city was experiencing a period of rapid growth. Businesses such as the Midelburg Theater, Smoke House Restaurant, and Pioneer Hotel became city landmarks in future years. (Courtesy of Bob Barker.)

On the morning of September 12, 1952, the city of Logan celebrated its 100th anniversary with the arrival of the official centennial train at the C&O Depot. Hundreds of residents were on hand to greet the steam engine. Later that afternoon at Midelburg Island, a C&O film exhibit commemorating the impact the local train yard made on the growth of the city was also held.

In 1936, the Triangle service station stood as the unofficial entrance to the city of Logan. The station offered Pepper gasoline and full service, and it featured Quaker State oil. In later years, the station became the location of a variety of restaurants, including Gino's, one of the city's first pizza parlors. Today, the building has been demolished, and the property displays an entrance sign to the city. Behind the filling station was the Water Street Bridge.

This aerial view of the thriving and growing community of Logan was taken in 1936. The belching smokestacks indicate the location of the Appalachian Electric Power Company powerhouse. At the time, the coal industry was booming within the county's boundaries, and the city was a bustling hub of activity.

The streets in the hustling business district at Stratton Street in downtown Logan were made of rough brick in the late 1920s. At the time, approximately 87,500 residents of varying nationalities were living in Logan County. Coal mining and coal-related industries were the predominant industries of the time. In 1926, more than 20.3 million tons of coal was mined in the county.

The Hurst & Harris store could be described as an early version of a department store. It sold dry goods, clothing, hardware, and groceries from its location on Main Street in downtown Logan. The city received funds to begin a street-paving project in 1914, though Main Street was still a dirt road in 1910 when this photograph of the store was taken.

These grade-school students attended classes in 1911 at a school later known as the Central Grade Building. As education advanced and the population flourished, more schools were established or expanded. By 1927, Logan County boasted 175 schools. The county had four senior high schools: one in Logan, one in Man, one in Sharples, and one in Aracoma. The 12 junior high schools were located throughout the county in Logan, Omar, Chapmanville, Holden, Ethel, Sharples, Man, Amherstdale, Lundale, Omar, Holden, and Aracoma.

This view from the 1920s depicts White Street between Cole and Dingess Streets in Logan. Miller Hardware & Supplies, Guyan Valley Wholesale, Aracoma Billiards, and several other prominent businesses were located on this back street, including a car dealership and tire shop. Even though most roads within the county's borders were still not yet surfaced, gasoline-powered cars were becoming a common site in the county. (Courtesy of Bob Barker.)

This photograph from the 1920s, taken by Carter's Studio, shows a portion of Dingess Street within the Logan city boundaries. By this time, this street and most other main thoroughfares in the city included sidewalks and brick-paved roadways. With the exception of the period automobiles, little has changed on this street when compared with today. (Courtesy of Bob Barker.)

The town of Chapmanville was founded in 1800 and named after Ned Chapman, an early settler. He was a local merchant who ran the first community post office. Over time, the development of the railroad brought accelerated growth to the town. The Chapmanville Depot was one of several whistle-stops in Logan County during the first decade of the 20th century. According to railroad historian Wib G. Whited, as stated in the *Centennial Program*, the first scheduled passenger train came to Logan Station in 1904. A single track stretched from Logan to Barboursville, passing through Chapmanville. Rails for the tracks were originally hauled down the Guyandotte River by push boats. The photograph below shows a scenic view of the town of Chapmanville in 1930.

After migrating from Italy to the United States in 1915, Joseph Nolletti worked and saved his earnings. On Christmas Day 1925, he opened City Bakery at 403 Stratton Street in Logan. Because few roads were paved at the time, bread trucks from larger cities like Charleston and Huntington were unable to deliver goods to the rural southern coalfields. Therefore, for many decades, City Bakery was nearly the sole provider of breads and bakery items to area restaurants and residents. The Nolletti family still owns the business.

This image from the early 1900s shows Mountain State Hardware Company, located on Main Street in Logan near Steele Furniture. The hardware store advertised electric and automobile supplies, mine equipment, and paints and oils. Besides independent stores, mine company stores were scattered throughout the coalfields. At such stores, miners purchased goods and services—groceries, hardware, toys, clothing, appliances, and furniture—with scrip (sometimes called script) issued to miners on payday. Scrip was issued as metal tokens or paper in different denominations, and it could only be used at specific stores affiliated with the mines that issued the scrip. (Courtesy of Karen Queen Cook and Mildred Queen.)

In the early 1920s, R. Bruce Harris (believed to be second from right in front of the hearse) owned Harris Undertaking Department, located above Logan Mercantile on Main Street in Logan. Harris was one of Logan's first undertakers. In 1909, he wrote that when beginning his career, he would travel to homes by horseback, carrying the instruments of his profession in saddlebags, and the body of the deceased would be prepared in the home. Later, he and his brother B.C. Harris owned and operated Harris Funeral Home.

Omar was a model community in the early 1930s. In a 2003 interview, local politician Raymond Chafin described the coal town: "It was a busy coalcamp with a large population. Besides hundreds of frame houses for miners and their families, there were larger homes for mine bosses. There were company-owned boardinghouses, a store, doctor's office, theater, church, and several large halls." (Courtesy of Bob Barker.)

This snapshot shows five officers of the West Virginia Mounted State Police from the Chapmanville Detachment of Company C and was likely taken in the early 1920s. Sgt. R.E. Brooks (center) was in charge of this detachment. For years, the state police maintained and utilized a mounted force to better navigate through the most rugged expanses of the county.

An ongoing offense through the decades in Logan County has been the illegal production of alcohol. Logan County's chief deputy, Earl Justice (far left), stands near Sheriff Okey Justice (wearing dark uniform). The third deputy, at right, is believed to be Garland Counts. The officers seized a copper still, barrels of homespun whiskey, and other distillery equipment during a bust in the early 1960s. (Courtesy of Mary Ryan Bainbridge.)

In this 1922 view taken near the current city of Logan post office, pictured from left to right are J.S. Mynes, C.W. Frazier, and L.E. "Chief" Thompson standing alongside the first telephone service motor vehicle in the county. From 1921 until the building was destroyed by fire on September 3, 1922, the telephone office was located in the White & Browning building. Replacement equipment was put into service in 1923 in a new facility on Hudgins Street.

This photograph from the 1880s is of the Alfred Buskirk family who lived in Aracoma (just outside Logan). Large families like this were commonplace during the period. The Buskirks were active in the early creation of the Aracoma Baptist Church. In 1891, Alfred was appointed as one of three trustees of the church and a delegate to the Guyandotte Association.

Dyke and Sallie Smith Garrett posed for this portrait when Dyke was approximately 70 years old. The couple resided in the Chapmanville area. Garrett, born in 1841, was known far and wide as an effective circuit-riding preacher responsible for organizing new churches in Logan and Mingo Counties. Over the course of his ministry, he preached numerous sermons at indoor and open-air revival services held around the territory. Garret also performed hundreds of local baptismal services. The first record of a baptism conducted by the preacher was published in the *Logan County Banner* in December 1889 and took place at Big Creek. Performing the baptism of Anderson "Devil Anse" Hatfield in 1911 was one of his proudest achievements, as the minister quipped afterwards to a young friend, saying that he had "successfully baptized the devil." During the Civil War, Garrett was a soldier in the Confederate army, and after the war, he and Devil Anse were members of Camp Straton United Confederate Veterans. Garrett died on May 29, 1938. (Courtesy of the Coleman C. Hatfield collection.)

This 1925 street scene is of Barnabus, West Virginia. The community was a typical coal camp where the town was owned and maintained by the coal mine. During this period, most residents worked in the deep mines or at mine-related industries nearby. Today, the area near Omar remains a somewhat heavily populated and scenic part of Logan County.

The two-story Accoville School provided educational opportunities to the youngsters of Triadelphia District in 1916. Coal operators who developed the community at the time of the first coal boom erected the school for the children of their employees. As with most schools and homes of the era, cast-iron coal heaters warmed the facility during the winter months. (Courtesy of Jack Cyfers.)

In the 1920s, the Great Atlantic & Pacific Tea Company (A&P Market) was located on Dingess Street at the Stratton Street intersection in Logan. Besides offering grocery items and a butcher shop, the store also carried hardware items and included a barbershop and beauty parlor. Across the street were the popular Midelburg Theater and the Louis Place, advertised as the "working man's store." (Courtesy of Bob Barker.)

According to historian G.T. Swain in his 1927 book *History of Logan County*, the First National Bank of Logan began business on April 2, 1906, in a small, one-room frame building that stood on part of the Bevill Hardware site. The bank opened with a capital stock of $50,000. By 1907, construction began on the three-story building shown here and located on Stratton Street near the original wooden structure.

This image, taken from a nearby hillside, depicts the community of West Logan in the early 1930s. In the background, the Guyandotte River meanders along the border of the community. On the opposite side of the river is the Peach Creek train yard and roundhouse and the YMCA building. The small town of Peach Creek can be seen in the far distance.

This image from 1921 shows the Island Creek Coal community of Holden. It appeared in an issue of *Pioneer Magazine*, a periodical published by the coal company in the early 1920s. At the time, Island Creek touted Holden as a model all-inclusive camp, offering fine homes, manicured yards, white picket fences, an opera house, a church, a meeting hall, and company stores. (Courtesy of Joe Hensley.)

Monitor Drive-In Theatre was once an especially popular hangout for Logan County teenagers. This photograph of the drive-in entrance was taken in 1955, during the theatre's heyday. Shown below is a photograph of Logan Auto Parts from 1955. It was located in Ellis Addition near the current location of Baisden Brothers Hardware Store. Logan Auto Parts offered a wide assortment of automobile parts, tires, and accessories. It was also a hangout for local residents who wanted to discuss the latest car models, vehicle features, or mechanical tips. An advertisement from the time said, "Does that hot rod of yours need a face lift? Then, come to Logan Auto Parts."

Pushboats, sometimes called flatboats, were a common form of transportation along the Guyandotte River throughout the 19th and early 20th centuries. They were flat-bottomed, rectangular crafts that traveled into Logan from as far as the Ohio River. This scene from approximately 1885 was taken near Ferrellsburg. Pushboats were used to transport heavy freight, and many early settlers first came to the area by way of these boats.

The Bolivar McDonald family, shown in this photograph from the 1880s, was one of the most prominent lineages in Logan. The McDonalds, along with the Harveys, Vinsons, Altizers, and Nighberts, bought or leased large tracts of land during this period and benefited greatly from their acquisitions. Local historian Robert Y. Spence once wrote that the first pioneer families to settle in the area included the McDonalds, Chambers, Browns, Hinchmans, and Claypools.

Elijah "Eli" White and his family casually pose for this image. Eli's ancestors were among the first to conquer the wilderness and settle in the region. By the 1880s, Eli owned a small farm near Cherry Tree. Farming was not an easy vocation for anyone in the southeastern reaches of West Virginia during this period. Suitable farmland or pastureland was difficult to come by, and level property was rare and expensive. For the common man, affordable acreage was mountainous and, oftentimes, still untouched wilderness. Cultivating the soil and raising crops demanded the aid of a stout mule or oxen team, and most work on the farm was still done by hand implements and physical exertion. Farming knowledge was usually acquired by example, passed to the children as they worked the fields alongside their parents. By the end of the 19th century, Eli had planted orchards and begun to raise cattle in addition to his farm crops. Travel by horseback was still common in the territory during this period. Eli died in October 1931.

This photograph from 1912 illustrates the official gathering of members of the Camp Straton Confederate Veterans held in the Chapmanville area. Included among the members at the reunion are William Dyke Garrett (who is shown with a long white beard standing at center behind the squatting man) and Henry Clay Ragland, a distinguished lawyer and the publisher of the *Logan County Banner*. Ragland is to the right of Garrett.

The C&O Depot in Logan has been a center of activity and a favorite gathering place for the community since cargo and passenger trains began running regularly. When this photograph was taken—perhaps around 1910—merchants, postal workers, and others would bring horse- or mule-drawn wagons or even handcarts and wait in line to pick up incoming freight at the station, which is located near the current city hall building.

Positioned in the cradle of the rugged Appalachian Mountains, Logan County is a unique region, once mostly secluded due to its terrain and with a long-standing reputation for tough, tumultuous union uprisings, blood feuds, and political rivalries. Religious fervor and passionate politics have long walked hand-in-hand in this area, and Logan's political life has always been colorful and complicated. The region was once notorious for strong-willed candidates who would do whatever it took to win. The reputation for what some characterize as underhanded political shenanigans and clannish fights dates all the way back to the days of Devil Anse Hatfield. At least two of Anse's sons, Joe and Tennis, went into politics and later controlled Logan County elections for years. Election Day was always a time of extreme anxiety and expectancy. In this snapshot from a 1929 Election Day in Omar, four local individuals wait for news on the final election results from the precincts. J.D. Hatfield, as noted in the sign, was one of several candidates running for office that political season: "Hatfield Means Success!! Sincere!! and Capable!!"

This installment of the Logan High School Band, under the direction of Carl McElfresh, was featured in the *Centennial Program* put out for the city of Logan's 100th anniversary. In program, the band was described as, "One of West Virginia's Finest." Besides their typical school duties and musical presentations that year, the band performed for the centennial celebration, held September 10–13, 1952.

While celebrating Logan's 100th anniversary in 1952, the first outdoor production of *The Aracoma Story* was performed on Midelburg Island. Local resident Tom Godby played Boling Baker, while Mary Faith Cox played the coveted role of Princess Aracoma. Today, Aracoma Story, Inc., is a nonprofit community theater company that produces several outdoor productions annually, including *The Aracoma Story*, at the Liz Spurlock Amphitheater at Chief Logan State Park.

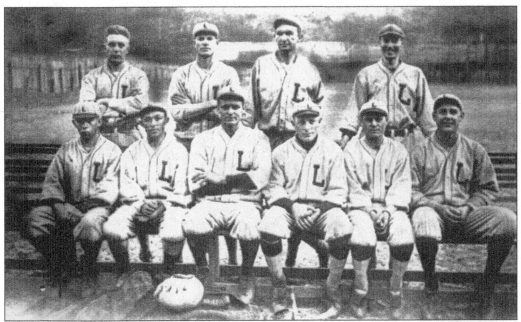

The first recorded baseball game in the county took place on May 30, 1889. The game was played in the town of Logan Courthouse (now the city of Logan). By the turn of the century, America's favorite pastime grew in local popularity. Most towns, coal mine operations, and coal camps had organized teams, and local competition became fierce. The above photograph shows an Logan team from the 1890s. The photograph below represents the 1929 installment of the Logan team. Ford Motor Company's Fordson tractors sponsored these players. Ball games were played in designated fields across the county. Well-attended rivalries developed over time among various neighborhoods, communities, and coal companies.

This photograph of the Guyan Valley Bank building on Stratton Street in Logan was taken in 1905. J. Cary Alderson organized the city's first bank on November 22, 1899, and it officially opened for business on January 1, 1900, in an 18-by-20-foot, one-room frame structure. The bank was first capitalized at $25,000 with a paid-in capital of $2,500. Guyan Valley Bank remained in its first facility until 1905, when the building shown was constructed at a cost of approximately $10,000. Blair Law Offices is now located where the bank once stood. The photograph below shows Dingess Street in Logan around 1907. Even though the street had not yet been paved, the sidewalks had already been constructed. Within a few years, brick paving would be added to most of the roadways within the city limits.

In the above snapshot, Grady Yeager, a relative of retired Maj. Gen. Chuck Yeager, stands beside his airplane in 1935; it was the first locally owned aircraft in the county. Grady Yeager went on to teach many local residents to fly. In the photograph below, Grady's sister Lillian Yeager is shown. She learned to fly at age nine, becoming the youngest recorded pilot in the region. In 1946, after an official inspection by Col. Hubert Stark, the state aeronautics chief at the time, the Logan Airfield opened for business. It was located across the river from Taplin, nine airline miles from the city of Logan. Later, a charter was issued by the state to the Logan Aircraft Service, Inc., with the incorporators listed as Grady Yeager, Bernard Shell Jr., and Robert Shell.

West Virginia Supermarkets was a small local chain of community grocery stores when this picture of its Ellis Addition location was taken in 1952. There were also store locations in West Logan and Man. Below, the Logan National Bank opened its doors in 1906, with one employee, Naaman Jackson. The bank was located in this one-room, one-story frame structure on Stratton Street in Logan. The officers included Scott Justice, president; S.A. Draper, vice president; Naaman Jackson, cashier; and the following board of directors: W.R. Lilly, H. Ewart, H.H. Morris, J.M. Mitchell, S.B. Lawson, Scott Justice, and S.A. Draper. Logan National Bank's name was changed to the First National Bank of Logan in 1908. The First National Bank of Logan eventually absorbed Logan's oldest banking institution, Guyan Valley Bank, in 1931.

The Peck Hotel, originally erected in the city of Logan by the Peck family in the 1870s, was a favorite overnight stop in Logan for travelers and tourists and a home for several full-time residents when the photograph above was taken in the 1880s. Later, in 1912, it was purchased from the family by businessmen S.B. Lawson and J.E. McDonald. The new owners remodeled the establishment in 1915. By 1922, the hotel was demolished to make way for a new railroad depot in Logan. The Peck family appears in the photograph below. They were respected and influential at the time this picture was taken in the 1890s. It was common for traveling photographers to appear in neighborhoods in the spring and summer months to take such family portraits.

The early portrait at left is of seven pioneer sisters. The photograph may have been taken in the early 1870s. Sitting in the first row, from left to right, are Leanor Hicks, Jane Whitman, and Susie McNeely. Standing in the second row, from left to right, are Elizabeth Altizer, Patsy Conley, Minerva White, and Nancy Altizer. Around the same time this photograph was taken, Florence Peck Adams wrote, "I remember Logan County as a very barren place to live. Most of the homes were built of logs and the cracks daubed with clay. The chimneys were built of native stone and clay." (Courtesy of Barbara Kovach Morris.)

Farabell Vance Morris and her husband, Mart Morris, pose in front of their Whitman home in the 1890s. (Courtesy of Barbara Kovach Morris.)

The appearance of the Guyan Valley train was always reason for increased activity during the last decade of the 19th century at the Logan Depot. It was backbreaking work for laborers to move heavy freight from the wooden train cars. Supplies and products were then loaded into waiting buckboards and wagons for eventual transport throughout the county. (Courtesy of Joe Hensley.)

In 1913, these coal miners stand at the portal of Logan Coal Company in Ethel. The employees include, from left to right, a Mr. Richardson, carman; Cleve Craddock, carpenter; C.W. Small, motorman; Lou Davis, mine foreman; Asbury Stidham, blacksmith; and Jerry Stidham, brakeman.

In 1950, with its extremely busy and prosperous business district, Logan was one of the state's fastest growing communities. Even though the boulevard had not yet been fully constructed, and traffic flow could occasionally be described as a nightmare, crowds of people still flocked to downtown, especially on the weekends.

The miners and developers who appear in this 1915 setting were responsible for opening up the Omar coalfields. Shown, from left to right, are (first row) Kelley Barker, John Easley, Mr. Hopkins, H.C. Dudley, Bill Jones, Mr. Stidle, Mr. Browning, and Mr. Greshman; (second row) Johnny Mosko, unidentified, Henry Crickman, Mr. Finger, Jim Montgomery, unidentified, Ray Barlow, A.J. Dalton, Abe Wood, Cap Dower, Tennis Hatfield (son of Devil Anse), and Bob French.

Members of the Loyal Order of Moose Lodge No. 902 gathered in front of the Logan County Courthouse for this group shot. The period was likely around 1914 or 1915. The third person from the left in the first row is Devil Anse Hatfield, leader of the feuding Hatfields.

The city of Logan placed an order for a new, state-of-the-art fire truck in the summer of 1921. By autumn 1922, the Logan Pumper was ready for its final evaluations. The truck, ordered from Winther Motors, underwent its preliminary pumping test at the time this picture was taken. The fire truck was then painted and shipped from Kenosha, Wisconsin, to the City of Logan Fire Department on Monday, November 6, 1922. (Courtesy of Bob Barker.)

Around 1915, most communities within the county had small marching bands. The Logan Military Band, originally assembled as a traveling cornet band, performed at special functions around the area and promoted the military draft. The band was first organized in 1892 in the town of Logan Courthouse, now the city of Logan.

After the county's first courthouse was destroyed in 1864, a brick courthouse was built in 1870 and remained until 1904, when it was demolished and a stone building was erected. In 1911, the new building caught fire and burned. Afterwards, the picturesque Logan County Courthouse, shown above in 1917, was completed at a cost of around $63,000. It remained until the early 1960s, when the current courthouse in Logan was built.

After selling his one-third interest in Logan Hospital, Dr. S.B. Lawson formed an enterprise and eventually built Logan General Hospital. Several owners followed Lawson. In 1947, the hospital was sold to Dr. W.E. Brewer, under whose leadership it remained for many years. The photograph at right was taken in 1952. Logan General Hospital was at the same location as the current Logan Regional Medical Center on Hospital Drive. The 1909 image below depicts an operation underway at Logan Hospital, better known as the old Mercy Hospital or the Guyan Valley Hospital. The two doctors shown are H.H. Farley (left) and L.E. Steele, pioneer physicians in the region and stockholders in Logan Hospital.

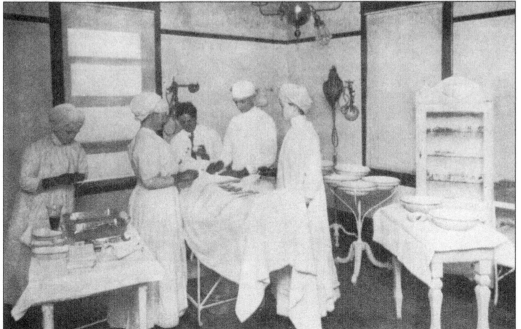

In this photograph from the 1950s, Mercy Hospital was located on Dingess Street in Logan. It was first established in 1906 as Logan Hospital. By 1908, Dr. H.H. Farley moved to Logan County. That same year, Dr. Farley joined with Dr. L.E. Steele, and both became major stockholders in the organization, and they led the medical facility for many years. The brick building was constructed in 1914.

In the early 1950s, local telephone operators for Southern Bell Telephone & Telegraph Company included, from left to right, June Creger, Faye Rorrer, and Effie Johnson. Operators held hectic positions, as they assisted over 7,000 subscribers at the time, providing information and assisting with local and long distance calls. By the mid-1950s, there were more than 700 miles of open telephone wire and 50 miles of aerial cable within the county's boundaries.

Converted to Christianity under the ministry of Alexander "Daddy" Lunsford during the time of the Civil War, Dyke "Uncle Dyke" Garrett, shown above, acted upon his calling and eventually became a circuit-riding preacher and evangelist. Garrett enlisted as a Confederate in the Logan Wildcats (Company D, 36th Virginia Infantry) around the beginning of the war. After it was discovered he was deaf in one ear, he became the company's unofficial chaplain. Upon his return to Logan County, he spent the rest of his life traveling throughout the region, spreading the gospel message and establishing several churches, including Crooked Creek Church of Christ. Garrett married Sallie "Aunt Sallie" Smith in 1867, and they remained married for 71 years. Friends Devil Anse Hatfield and Dyke Garrett were members of Camp Straton United Confederate Veterans, a social organization that influenced local politics for over 45 years beginning in 1870.

Baptismal services are being held along the Guyandotte River in Accoville, West Virginia, in this tattered photograph taken March 30, 1919. Family members and church faithful gathered along the banks of the river to support the young believer who was preparing to be immersed. It is likely that several individuals were baptized on this day. Faith and church attendance remain important components of Logan County culture, and outdoor and indoor baptismal services remain commonplace. (Courtesy of Michael Taylor.)

This large Sunday school class assembled in front of what is believed to be the Logan Methodist Church for this portrait in the mid-1890s. A.J. Coffey, a pioneer minister in Logan County, once wrote that records indicated Methodists first established a church in Logan in 1825. Other denominations followed and were established, including the Christian church in 1868, the Baptist church in 1891, the Presbyterian church in 1907, the Catholic church in 1911, the B'nai El congregation in 1918, the Episcopal church in 1924, and the Church of the Nazarene in 1935.

The Gospel Four was a southern gospel singing group popular in Logan County during the late 1940s and 1950s. They included, from left to right, Bernard Hopkins, Maywood Williams, Jean Williams, D.W. "Bit" Hinchman, and pianist Bobby Ghee. They often performed at the Logan Armory (now Plaza Lanes), at local churches, and live on the radio. Hinchman was later choir director at McConnell Tabernacle and Sunbeam Chapel. (Courtesy of Cheryl R. Davis.)

The men's Bible class assembled on June 5, 1927, outside Central Christian Church on Stratton Street in downtown Logan for this official photograph. Hunter's Studio, a local photography business, documented the meeting on film. The church is now called First Christian Church of Logan. (Courtesy of the First Christian Church of Logan.)

This threadbare Wildcat flag, on display at the West Virginia Cultural Center in Charleston, represents an important piece of Logan history. Historian G.T. Swain penned in 1927 that the Logan Wildcats played a conspicuous part in the Civil War and were fearless fighters. The 11 white stars of the flag represented the 11 states that had withdrawn from the Union to form a new nation. The 12 and largest star symbolizes the state of West Virginia and its Southern sympathizers.

The McDonalds were one of the first pioneer families to settle in the region. As the coal and timber industries grew, land increasingly became an important commodity. The McDonald family became early landowners by purchasing or leasing large tracts of property; they found prosperity in the coal and timber fields of Logan. The McDonald brothers posing in this photograph were, from left to right, Matravers, Bolivar, Astynax, and Scott.

Wesley Toler, son of Riley and Minnie Toler, is shown riding a railway cycle in the early 1920s. Wesley worked for Mallory Coal Company. From the beginning of the rail system in Logan, railroad workers often used cycle cars like this to travel the rails and to inspect train tracks throughout the region. This particular style of pedal-operated cycle, made of tubular steel, has also been referred to as an inspection pedicycle or velocipede. In addition to railroad workers operating the contraptions, common residents occasionally used velocipedes for Sunday afternoon excursions through the countryside, and races have even been documented over the years. This activity continued even though railroad companies frowned on the practice. An article in the *Logan Democrat* from April 27, 1911, reported a velocipede had been spotted in use by a non-railroad worker on the local train tracks, despite objections from the railroad. (Courtesy of Jack Cyfers.)

It was a difficult way of life. Local miners are pictured at a coal tipple at the community of Landville, in the early 1900s when pickaxes and stout mules were used inside the mine and outside at the tipple. The coal miners, from left to right, are (shown on work mules) Cum Workman, Charlie Mullins, and Bob Blankenship; (background) Everett Hager, William Toler, and unidentified.

In 1955, one of the county's new car dealerships was Hartman Motor Company, located in Deskins Addition. The dealer featured Packard automobiles and a wide variety of used vehicles. Over the years, a variety of new and used automobile dealerships were situated in Deskins Addition, including Paul Cook Ford, Bob Compton Motors, Milne Pontiac, Aracoma Motors, Yeager Motors, Honeycutt Pontiac-Buick-GMC, and Mike Ferrell Toyota.

Locally owned and operated, Lilly's Crown Jewelers on Stratton Street was once one of Logan's most popular jewelry stores. The store offered a wide variety of engagement rings, gemstones, diamonds, necklaces, watches, clocks, radios, and gift items. As this photograph from the 1950s demonstrates, the store became especially hectic as the Christmas season approached. Crowds would form daily as demand for holiday gifts grew.

This photograph of Logan County deputies was taken in front of the Logan County Courthouse. The deputy standing at the center of the front row is Cap Hatfield, son of Devil Anse Hatfield. Cap Hatfield considered himself suited for law enforcement and was once described by his grandson, Coleman C. Hatfield, as a man not to be reckoned with. (Courtesy of the Coleman C. Hatfield collection.)

This is believed to be the first C&O Railway freight depot located in the city of Logan. By the time it was condemned by the city in 1916 and plans made for a larger facility, the depot had been a hub of activity for many years. On February 24, 1916, the *Logan Democrat* reported that the final plans for a new, expanded train depot had been made.

In 1955, Baisden service center was a busy, full-service automobile filling station in the Verdunville area. Siblings Jackie and Shirley Baisden pose outside the station. The business offered Gulf No-Nox gasoline and a variety of other products. It continued in Verdunville for many years.

Automobiles were first seen in Logan County around 1914. Since that time, many local dealerships have opened their doors for business to meet the growing consumer demand for both new and used vehicles. In the mid-1950s, at least two successful automobile dealers were located in the community of Stollings along the main drag, Route 10. Brumfield Motors, the county's Buick dealership, was positioned near the Stollings underpass. In more recent years, the location became the longtime home of Mike Ferrell Ford, another dealership, until the building was demolished in 2010. Minton Chevrolet was located nearby, just several doors down from another county landmark, Morrison's Drive-In Restaurant. Minton Chevrolet featured a full Chevy lineup, and in later years, the dealership became L&S Chevrolet and Oldsmobile. Eventually, it evolved into Thornhill GM Superstore, which is now located along US 119, Corridor G, in Chapmanville. The original structure that housed Minton Chevrolet is now occupied by Georgia Carpet and adjacent to Family Discount Pharmacy.

In 1921, Island Creek Coal Company maintained Whitman Boarding House as part of its camp community. House lodgers were employed by the mine and were oftentimes single. Miners would rent a room for weeks or months at a time. Besides the private bedrooms, there was a common room on the first floor for meals and fellowship. The boardinghouse was located in the coal camp. (Courtesy of Joe Hensley.)

In an article dated May 15, 1914, the *Logan County Banner* reported that motorcars were first seen and photographed locally at the First Baptist Church of Logan. From that point forward and throughout the decades, automobiles became popular and eventually plentiful. Aracoma Motors, Inc., shown in this 1955 picture, maintained a thriving automobile dealership in Deskins Addition. The business carried Chrysler and Plymouth products.

Two

Landmarks and Industry

For over 90 years, Aracoma Hotel remained one of Logan County's most beloved and magnificent landmarks. The hotel was erected in 1917 on Cole and Main Streets in downtown Logan under the leadership of Harvey Ghiz. It first opened its doors to the public in March 1918 and became the headquarters for many political gatherings over the years. In 1921, the hotel was the command center during the Blair Mountain War. A massive fire destroyed the hotel in 2010.

The Aracoma Hotel was named after a Shawnee princess. As shown in this photograph from the early 1920s, the Aracoma Hotel stood as the cornerstone of the community. Over time, its historic guest registry included such luminaries as Devil Anse Hatfield, Cap Hatfield, John F. Kennedy, Robert Kennedy, Edward Kennedy, Roy Rogers, Gabby Hayes, and Lorne Greene. An accidental fire took place on November 15, 2010, destroying the fourth floor of the landmark. Within days, a corner of the remaining structure collapsed, and a final demolition of the remaining building was ordered thereafter. At the time of the fire, one Logan County historian said, "The heart of Logan is broken and a precious piece of West Virginia history has been lost forever."

This early depiction of the city of Logan, first published on a full-color postcard, showed a view looking down Stratton Street from the vantage point of the Jefferson Street intersection. On the left stands the Guyan Valley Bank building, and on the right side of the image is the First National Bank of Logan.

U.B. Buskirk built this impressive home for his fiancée, having designed it for utility services he was sure would eventually come to Logan. He plumbed the home for water and gas and wired it for electricity. Water initially was obtained from a well by means of a windmill and later provided by a reservoir. The home was eventually sold to J.W. Hinchman, becoming known as the Hinchman Mansion.

The city of Logan looked much different in the 1890s when this picture was taken. It would still be years before the most common of utility services, indoor plumbing, or paved streets would arrive in the county seat. The church on the left side of the photograph is believed to be the Logan Northern Methodist Church.

This photograph shows an inside view of the Man Smoke House around 1948. The restaurant, located in downtown Man, was a favorite hangout among residents of Triadelphia District. Besides featuring a simple country menu and soft drinks, the establishment also had a public radio and pinball machines for entertainment. Seated in the booth is "Bones" Cook (right). The male waiter standing behind the counter was nicknamed "Jinks."

The timber and lumber business was one of the first successful, large-scale business enterprises in Logan County, beginning around 1876 at Crawley Creek. Conditions were extremely harsh for early timber workers, for it demanded arduous and dangerous efforts for relatively meager pay. In the woods near Crawley, the timber crew above includes, from left to right, (first row) John Smith, William H. Fugate, and John Dingess; (second row) Nath Whitt, Cush Dingess, Roosevelt Williams, Ervin Smith, and Harry Dingess. Shown below, logs, such as these from the Craneco log camp, were chain-hauled from the woods by mules or workhorses. Later, the logs were made into rafts and floated down the Guyandotte River to the Ohio River for processing.

One of the earliest timber crews in the Harts Creek region gathered at the logging camp after a long day of toil. By this period, workers had constructed splash dams. Damming up the mountain water enabled the logs to be transported out of the woods more efficiently. Besides the emerging timber business during the last half of the 19th century, farming was also an important occupation. In the photograph below, John Dingess, who had been a timber worker in his younger days, worked and maintained a family farm in Mount Gay by the 1880s. Dingess appears in the center with his son and grandson and holding to his team of mules.

In 1870, a new courthouse was constructed on Stratton Street in Logan County at the location of the old log courthouse. During the Civil War, the log structure was set ablaze by Federal troops led by Clinton Buskirk. The new brick building remained and served the people's needs until 1904, when it was demolished and a stone courthouse was erected. (Courtesy of the Coleman C. Hatfield collection.)

The Christian faith and church attendance were central to community life for many in the last half of the 19th century. During this era, Logan Methodist Church was located on Main Street in Logan next to what would later become Harris Funeral Home. In 1915, members of this fellowship held a cornerstone ceremony for a new building, Nighbert Memorial Methodist Church, which would be located on White Street.

After the Chesapeake & Ohio Railway Company (C&O) came to the county, changes began to occur in the lumber industry. Logs could now be transported via train tracks, as was the case at this logging operation at Lorado in 1910. The railways became a major factor in the advancement of the timber industry, and camps would follow along the C&O line.

According to a statement from local timber pioneer John Ferrell in the *Centennial Program*, the logging industry grew from mountain to mountain and creek to creek. In addition to the larger companies, there were smaller outfits—consisting of a small crew, pack mules, heavy chains, and bounteous determination—that could develop overnight. In the 1890s, these men were logging around the Stollings area, hauling hardwood from the high mountains. (Courtesy of the Coleman C. Hatfield collection.)

During the 1940s, a Labor Day political rally brought throngs of residents into Omar, West Virginia. The brand of politics found in the region has been described as colorful and entertaining. During this era, the Island Creek District and Omar were heavily populated with coal mine employees and their families who lived in a variety of coal camps.

The Peach Creek train yard was a major county employer for many years. In the 1950s, the shop track crew, at the wheel pit, included, from left to right, (first row) Arthur Ray, Charles Fleming, Max Wall, Johnny Eskins, Howard Johnson, and Reford Dingess; (second row) Franklin Noel, Paul Hale, Jessy Estep, Lyle Butcher, Clarence D. Stowers, Bill Faulkner, Bob Hale, Alderson Hale, Wayne Chafin, Earl White, and Waldo Hugel. (Courtesy of Earl White.)

The Dehue coal camp, located at Rum Creek, was similar in appearance to most camps that existed during the period. This image, taken in the 1940s, shows what was known as "first camp" at Dehue. The single-story households (white houses with green trim) were for coal mine employees and their families. The two-story homes were reserved for mine bosses. In the far distance are the company store and the Dehue Community Church.

This is a view of the main floor of Watson's Department Store in 1952. The store, which advertised itself at the time as Logan's newest and most up-to-date shopping center, was located on Stratton Street. Today, Peebles Department Store is in the same location, positioned across the street from the Logan Courthouse entrance.

Harris Funeral Home is considered one of Logan's chief landmarks, situated on Main Street. Although it had been in operation since 1909, Harris Funeral Home opened its doors at this location on September 6, 1931. Bruce Harris, one of Logan County's first undertakers, was the owner. The business is still in operation at this location and is now called Honaker Funeral Home.

The Doran Hinchman Mansion, one of the most striking of homes in Logan's city limits, had been built and wired for electricity in 1892. However, it took 13 years before electric lights became available in Logan (in 1905). Initially, electricity came from Atkinson-White Light Company and was only supplied from dark until 11:00 p.m. The Hinchman family purchased the home in 1913. Due to faulty wiring, it caught fire in 1976 and burned to the ground.

This 1952 view shows the three-story Island Creek Number One Store located in Holden, West Virginia. The company store provided employees of Island Creek Coal Company with a wide assortment of clothing, shoes, toys, furniture, appliances, and grocery items. The facility now houses the Appalachian Dream Center, a nonprofit ministry of Operation Compassion.

The Mallory Company Store, shown in 1951, was located in the community of Mallory and focused its trade on serving coal miners and their families. As with most company stores of the period, miners could buy on credit or use company-issued scrip to purchase all their household necessities.

Construction on Logan High School at the east end of Stratton Street began in 1921. Prior to construction, high school students attended classes at the Central Grade Building on the hill overlooking downtown Logan. The new school, shown above in the early 1950s, served students until it was replaced with the current campus on Midelburg Island in 1956. Below, for many years, the Chapmanville High School was a well-known structure positioned in the center of the town of Chapmanville. A gymnasium was being constructed at the time this photograph was taken in 1952. After the construction of the new high school in the 1960s, this facility became the junior high school until a new junior high was eventually built. Although it has since been demolished, many residents have fond memories of attending the old school.

This view of Man High School from the early 1950s likely kindles fond memories for many county residents and remains a landmark in the town of Man. For several decades, the school offered educational opportunities for many Triadelphia District students, first as the town of Man's sole high school and later as the junior high school. The building remains in the community, although it now stands vacant.

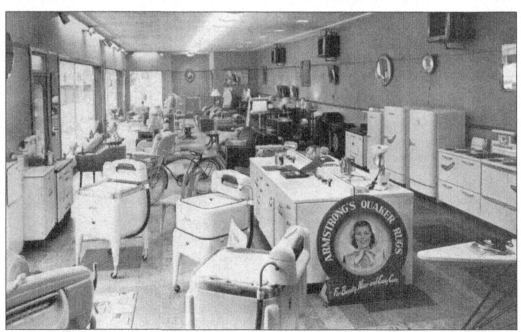

In 1951, when this interior photograph was taken, the Meade Furniture Company was known as a business "where quality reigns supreme." The store, which targeted coal miners and their families, was located in the town of Man and offered a variety of products, including home furnishings, small and major appliances, electronics, linoleum, and some sporting goods.

The first Island Creek Coal Company No. 1 Store opened for business in 1902 and was located along the railroad tracks near Copperas Mine Fork, where the town of Holden was being built. The territory surrounding Holden was mostly farmland or still covered by timber at the time Island Creek Coal Company opened up mines in the region. During the next 10 years, Holden and other camps nearby grew rapidly.

This artist's rendering was developed for a proposed Holden High School building. By 1921, the project was approved and construction was well underway. From the time Island Creek Coal Company started developing the coal town of Holden, an instantaneous population explosion directly related to the booming coal industry ensued. In less than 20 years since the town began, a high school was required in Holden due to student numbers. (Courtesy of Joe Hensley.)

The Main Island Creek Coal Company first came to Logan in 1902. By 1903, local residents Thomas Harvey, S.S. Altizer, George F. Miller, and Vicie Nighbert sold approximately 37,000 acres of land on Island Creek, which was at the mouth of Pine Creek, to Clinton Cole and Omar Crane for the sum of $260,000. Cole and Crane were timber dealers and were interested in the logging resources on the property. The land they purchased was later sold to Island Creek Coal Company. By the early 1950s, Island Creek Coal Company had become a massive organization with a huge workforce and a variety of mine sites in Island Creek and Main Holden. The Island Creek Coal Company No. 7 (above) and No. 28 (below) Mines were active coal tipples in the county for many years.

One of downtown Logan's most celebrated eateries was the Smoke House Restaurant, located at 134 Stratton Street. In this image from the 1950s, owner Albert Klele Sr. stands at the cash register. In its heyday, the restaurant quickly filled to standing-room-only capacity by the lunch hour. While campaigning in Logan in 1960, Sen. John F. Kennedy and his brothers often dined at the Smoke House.

In the late 1960s and throughout the 1970s, the Smoke House continued as Logan's favorite hangout. Gus and Irene Glavaris and Sam Murredu owned the diner at this time. In an interview in 2002, Claude Ellis, who had purchased the business in the 1980s, described it: "County politicians and city businessmen congregated daily at the restaurant. Over the years, thousands of political deals and business transactions have taken place at the Smoke House.

This 1951 image is of the C.G. Steele Company, better known by most residents simply as Steele Furniture Store. The furniture, television, stereo, and appliance business was located on Main Street in downtown Logan across from McCormick's Department Store. The store manager during the period was Jack Johnson. The business continued operating into the 1980s.

In the 1920s, Junior Mercantile Company was a center of activity for the residents of the coal town of Earling between Logan and Man. Besides carrying a full line of products from home furnishings and clothing to grocery items, Junior Mercantile also featured pool tables, a snack bar, and public radio for the entertainment of the community. (Courtesy of the Coleman C. Hatfield collection.)

At one time, the C&O train yard, with its complex series of parallel tracks and roundhouse, was one of the largest and most active railroad yards in the state. The popular YMCA building, which was frequented by railroad employees, was located across from the train yard near the community of Peach Creek.

After an earlier Logan County Courthouse building burned in 1911, the Falls City Construction Company won the bid to build a new facility, and construction began soon thereafter. The massive structure was completed in 1913—an impressive example of post–Civil War architecture—and served the people of Logan County for the next 50 years. This image of the courthouse entrance was taken in 1952.

By 1921, the community of Holden had long been known as Main Island Creek Coal Company's model coal town. Among the facilities available to mine employees were the opera house and bandstand shown here. The community also had several assembly halls, a community church, and a company store. Bordered by white picket fences, individual yards were immaculately manicured, and camp houses were painted annually. Below, this close-up image from the 1940s shows a train car being loaded with bituminous coal at the Peach Creek coal tipple. Once the cars were loaded, they would be moved onward to the train yard. (Above, courtesy of Joe Hensley; below, courtesy of Bob Barker.)

For years, the Logan Depot was a place of constant motion. Steam-powered coal and freight trains stopped or passed through Logan on an hourly basis, and passenger trains transported people to and from the heart of the city. This particular scene from 1920 depicts the flood of activity that was part of daily life along the Logan tracks.

This image from 1932 shows the city of Logan at its zenith; business was thriving and the sidewalks were crowded with shoppers. Employment was up and establishments such as Guyan Valley Bank, State Restaurant, Lewis Furniture, Beckett Furniture, Pioneer Hotel, Smoke House Restaurant, Aracoma Hotel, and Midelburg Theater were experiencing a time of prosperity due to the boom in the local coal industry. (Courtesy of Tim and Susie Hiroskey.)

This 1908 photograph, which was taken in the community of Holden, shows of one of the first steam engines traveling through the county. At the time, the community of Holden was less than five years old, and the railroad system was in its earliest stages. The first train began running through Logan County on the Guyandotte Valley Railway lines in 1903, transforming the coal and timber industry in southern West Virginia.

By the first decade of the 20th century, Omar was a large municipality with a well-developed infrastructure for the period. Electrical service even came early to Omar, produced by Island Creek Coal's own power plant. In addition to providing ample housing, the company also developed a complex of community buildings and halls, including Omar Graded Public School, Omar Community Church, Miners Bath House, and Omar Auditorium.

In 1905, this crew of carpenters began early construction on E.R. Johnson Coal Company houses at Crooked Creek. A company-operated power plant was also erected. Later, in the November 28, 1907, edition of the *Fayette Journal*, an article was published documenting the organization of the E.R. Johnson Coal Company in the county. By then, homes were ready to be occupied, and the mine was ready to begin its operation.

Like many coal camps in the county, the community of Ethel grew up nearly overnight, established in the first decade of the 20th century. By the 1920s, when this image was taken, the area was heavily populated with homes reserved mostly for coal company employees and their families. This structure was Ethel Grade School, a two-story frame building that offered educational opportunities for the children in the camp. (Courtesy of John Szucs.)

An observance, which included the participation of many visiting dignitaries from across the state and the official laying of the Masonic cornerstone, took place on October 10, 1923. The formal ceremony dedicated the handsome new Logan Masonic Lodge facility on lower Main Street.

The Club House, erected by Island Creek Coal Company, was an ornate structure situated in the community of Omar, first designed and maintained for the pleasure and comfort of corporate representatives, coal mine foremen, and traveling dignitaries. Once heavily staffed with service workers, the facility offered its tenants and visitors spacious rooms for lodging, dining halls, billiard tables, and other amenities.

Once a famous structure in southern West Virginia, this is the Anderson "Devil Anse" Hatfield home. It is located at Sarah Ann on Main Island Creek in Logan County. The image, likely taken in the 1890s, was labeled to indicate where the springhouse and ginseng garden were situated on the estate. Although the home no longer stands, the Hatfield family cemetery overlooks the old home-site property from a nearby mountain.

Bevill's Hardware & Furniture Store, once a mainstay in downtown Logan, originally opened its doors for business on Main Street in 1904. Shown in this photograph, the new facility was later constructed on Stratton Street next to the First National Bank of Logan building, which now houses the Audiology and Hearing Aid Center and Don Browning's Jewelers (and previously housed Kopy Kat and Aracoma Drug).

Reminiscent of the times of Huckleberry Finn, this image depicts a period prior to 1900 when transportation sometimes involved employing a ferry service or renting a horse. This ferry transport enterprise was located near Plaza Lanes in Logan, approximately where the steel railroad bridge is now located. Walter McNeely (left) and John Gillespie push the raft forward with long poles as they maneuver to the riverbank to accommodate another customer. During the same period, the first public highway system was already established in Logan. Travelers were able to rent horses from a stable at Mounts Addition in Logan and ride them to Dingess, where they could leave the horses for others to ride back to Logan. These specialized forms of transportation mostly concluded after 1904, when the Chesapeake & Ohio Railroad (C&O) came to the area. By 1916, motorized taxies ran between Holden and Omar and other locations—as long as the roads were dry and the creeks were not too deep.

Legendary outdoorsman, Confederate guerilla fighter, landowner, businessman, and family patriarch Devil Anse Hatfield garnered international attention for his involvement in the infamous Hatfield and McCoy feud. Born in Logan County to Ephraim and Nancy Vance Hatfield on September 9, 1839, Devil Anse died at his Main Island Creek home on January 6, 1921, at the age of 81. Hundreds of local residents gathered afterwards to mourn his passing and to attend his solemn funeral. Today, perhaps the most recognizable memorial landmark in the county is the graveyard statue of the feudist. This imposing carving, which was erected shortly after his death, was made of Italian Carrara marble. Besides acknowledging the burial place of the famous Hatfield family patriarch, the statue's base also lists the names of Devil Anse's 13 children and of his wife, Louvicey Chafin Hatfield, most of whom were participants in the family vendetta. The cemetery is located on a mountaintop near the property where his home once stood on Route 44 at Sarah Ann.

Island Creek Coal Company's Store No. 1 was located in the coal camp community of Main Holden. Erected around 1903, the company store was considered a state-of-the-art facility and served company employees and families. It featured grocery items, a butcher shop, hardware items, clothing, home furnishings, a barbershop, and major appliances for its customers.

Louvicey Hatfield, the grieving widow of Devil Anse Hatfield, and other immediate family members assemble to honor and remember the feud leader on the mountaintop at the Hatfield family cemetery shortly after a statue of the feudist was erected at his gravesite in January 1921. The Italian marble carving is mentioned on the National Register of Historic Places. (Courtesy of Raamie Barker.)

Three

HEADLINES AND THE FAMOUS

Considered to be among the famous of Logan County, the Hatfield clan was living on Beech Fork of the Tug River when this likeness was made around 1888. Cap Hatfield, perhaps the most ferocious of the feud participants, is shown in the second row at the extreme right with his rifle. Patriarch Devil Anse and wife, Louvicey, are second and third from the left in the second row. (Courtesy of the Coleman C. Hatfield collection.)

This image from the 1880s depicts Devil Anse Hatfield and others as they pose for an unknown photographer before a scheduled hunting expedition. Shown from left to right are Ellison Mounts, Devil Anse Hatfield, Jim Vance, and a man named Borden, who arranged for the photography session. (Courtesy of the Coleman C. Hatfield collection.)

This image of Willis Hatfield was taken in the early 1970s. Son of Devil Anse Hatfield, Willis was once a Logan County deputy, working with and for his brothers who were also law enforcement officers. At the time this picture was taken, Willis was nationally known as one of the remaining offspring of the feud patriarch; he lived quietly in the first camp of the coal camp community of Dehue.

This is the earliest known image of Devil Anse Hatfield, who would have been 30–40 years old when an unknown photographer took this portrait. He was born in Logan County, the son of Ephraim and Nancy Hatfield, on September 9, 1839. The well-worn likeness was found among the personal belongings of his wife, Louvicey "Vicey" Hatfield, along with an album of other photographs and tintypes of her immediate family. The era when this image was made would have been several years following the Civil War. By this time, he was already a successful farmer, landowner, and timberman, but he was still unknown to the rest of the world. Within a few years, however, his name and the story of the family vendetta would make worldwide headlines. It is said that Randal McCoy, enemy of the Hatfield patriarch, once described Devil Anse as "six feet of devil and 180 pounds of hell." Over time, five of McCoy's children lost their lives to the feud. (Courtesy of the Coleman C. Hatfield collection.)

This image was made at a more peaceful time for the Hatfield clan, long after the feud violence subsided. Devil Anse and Louvicey are in the front row with young Alie Hatfield. In the second row are, from left to right, unidentified, Tennis, Joe, Willis, and Elizabeth Hatfield. (Courtesy of the Coleman C. Hatfield collection.)

Joe Hatfield, son of Devil Anse and Louvicey Hatfield, sits behind the driver's seat of this early-20th-century jalopy. The passenger is unidentified. Interested in business and local government, Hatfield, a Republican, ran for sheriff of Logan County in 1928 and continued to dabble in local politics through the 1930s and 1940s. (Courtesy of the Coleman C. Hatfield collection.)

According to Coleman C. Hatfield, the great-grandson of Devil Anse Hatfield, it was no accident that the *New York World* was the first national newspaper to take notice and report the feud, nor was it happenstance that the popular image of the hillbilly was fixed by illustrations that accompanied the article. However, Devil Anse was anything but a common hillbilly despite being raised in a rugged, pioneer region. Soon after the Civil War, Anse began acquiring property and became a successful timberman, farmer, and entrepreneur. He was so successful that in 1911, *Life Magazine* depicted him in a caption as "rich and religious." Yet those who knew him best described Anse as an outstanding rifle shot, competent outdoorsman, accomplished hunter, and exceptional horseman. In the biography *Tale of the Devil*, Coleman C. Hatfield wrote that Devil Anse maintained a special bond with "horseflesh" and a love for the Appalachian Mountains throughout his life. (Courtesy of the Coleman C. Hatfield collection.)

Shown in more detail than on the cover, this photograph depicts Mayor McGuire on horseback during a parade celebrating Logan's centennial. In a 1952 public letter written prior to the festivities, McGuire wrote, "To Almighty God we give thanks for the 100 years of bountiful life that has been ours, and to our forefathers, we pay homage for the rich heritage they have given us."

In the fall of 1911, Devil Anse Hatfield chose to make peace with God and was baptized by William Dyke Garrett in the creek near the Hatfield home at Sarah Ann. Garrett, shown sitting on the creek bank in the first row, considered the baptismal service one of the highlights of his ministry.

This photograph depicts another likeness of the seemingly tired leader of the well-known family vendetta. Several years after the death of Devil Anse Hatfield, historian G.T. Swain wrote about the post-feud era in his 1927 manuscript, *History of Logan County*: "Those days of lawlessness and strife are gone forever and not one of the living actors would ever have it to return. As they draw near to the evening tide of life, they would like to blot from memory's pages those dreadful dark days of strife, and look to better deeds." It's likely that Devil Anse harbored certain regrets toward the end of his life concerning the dark years of the feud, yet it's also believed that he found peace in his twilight years. (Courtesy of Robert Y. Spence and the Coleman C. Hatfield collection.)

It was a wild and woolly time in Logan's history. Willis Hatfield, son of Devil Anse, could be an intimidating figure when armed. He was a deputy at the time this image was made. Years later, in an off-duty incident, Willis was arrested for his involvement in a killing. An article in the *Fayette Tribune* from January 4, 1912, reported: "Willis Hatfield of Herberton emptied all six chambers of his pistol into the body of Dr. E.O. Thornhill, . . . killing him instantly. Hatfield had been drinking, . . . and his supply of whiskey ran down." Willis was infuriated when the doctor refused to write him a prescription for more drugstore whiskey. In anger, he drew his revolver and shot. Hatfield was jailed at Pineville. When the case went to trial, his brother Cap assisted in his defense. After deliberation, the jury charged Willis with murdering Dr. Thornhill, returning a verdict of voluntary manslaughter. Judge Miller sentenced Hatfield to serve four years in the penitentiary. Willis served his time peacefully and returned home, living the rest of his life in a private manner. (Courtesy of the Coleman C. Hatfield collection.)

Heavily armed and united, this view of the Hatfield clan includes, from left to right, (first row) Tennis Hatfield, Devil Anse Hatfield, and Willie Hatfield; (second row) Ock Damron, Elias Hatfield, Troy Hatfield, Rose Hatfield (standing in the doorway), Joe Hatfield, Cap Hatfield, and W.C. Border. Louvicey Hatfield is sitting behind everyone on the porch. (Courtesy of the Coleman C. Hatfield collection.)

A tragic American love story, Roseanna McCoy is shown in this haunting image when she was around 20 years old. She was once loved but later scorned by Johnson "Johnse" Hatfield. It's believed that at the time of the abandonment Roseanna was pregnant. The incident soon escalated the tensions between the two clans. (Courtesy of the Coleman C. Hatfield collection.)

Dr. Coleman C. Hatfield described his grandfather, Cap Hatfield (shown in the photograph), as constantly being wary from being hunted most of his adult life due to actions related to the feud. Coleman explained, "It did not take much to make him suspicious to the point of being paranoid." Cap believed he would eventually be transported to Kentucky against his will to stand trial over feud atrocities. By the time this photograph was taken, Cap had long proved he could be an extremely violent man if cornered. At the same time, he was also interested in furthering his education, and in middle age, he earned his law degree and influenced his children to go to college. Coleman A. Hatfield, his son, became a respected Logan County attorney. During the 1920s, Cap became involved in several business enterprises and interested in law enforcement, serving as a Logan County deputy. In August 1930, after a short illness, Cap died in a Baltimore hospital. (Courtesy of the Coleman C. Hatfield collection.)

Johnse Hatfield created much suffering for the Hatfield family. From the beginning, he had an undeniable eye for women and a taste for homespun whiskey. Both, on numerous occasions, got him into trouble. Although Johnse may have met and spoken with Roseanne McCoy prior to the Pikeville, Kentucky, election in August 1880, it was at that time the couple defied their families and went away to share private hours. Through a series of related circumstances, Johnse took Roseanne home, but they were refused permission to marry. Unwelcome at the Hatfield homestead or at her own home, Roseanne moved in with the Jim Vance family. Jim was Devil Anse's uncle. She and Johnse continued to see each other for the next year, but Johnse eventually lost interest in the relationship. Tragically, at the time Johnse abruptly ended the doomed courtship, Roseanne was pregnant with his child. She died soon thereafter of pneumonia coupled with a broken heart, and he later married her cousin, Nancy McCoy. (Courtesy of the Coleman C. Hatfield collection.)

Family, friends, and the curious gathered at the Anderson Hatfield family home at Island Creek to mourn the passing of the famous family patriarch. The day was January 6, 1921, and it was documented that over 5,000 mourners visited the farmhouse at Sarah Ann to show their respects—the largest peaceful assembly of its kind to date in the area. (Courtesy of the Coleman C. Hatfield collection.)

During the funeral service held in January 1921, Devil Anse Hatfield's immediate family surrounded his casket to say their goodbyes. Hatfield can be seen lying in state. Nan and Cap Hatfield stand immediately behind the coffin at the center of the group. The obituary was later published in the local newspaper in the January 14 issue of the *Logan County Banner*. (Courtesy of the Coleman C. Hatfield collection.)

Robert F. Kennedy meets with Alex DeFobio and Claude "Big Daddy" Ellis while campaigning for brother Sen. John F. Kennedy in Logan County in 1960. Ellis, a local Democratic factional boss, was the chairman of the local John F. Kennedy for President campaign, while DeFobio, a local theater operator, was a strong supporter of the Kennedys.

Building an inheritance of faith, these pioneer preachers became famous locally for spreading the good news and for cultivating churches. Dyke Garrett (left) poses with J. Green McNeely and A.J. Coffey (right). According to Coffey in the 1952 *Centennial Program*, "While Logan people are largely true to old time convictions, religious hatreds are not prevalent, and a fine spirit of Christian fellowship permeates all groups."

As a small child, Coleman A. Hatfield would often sit on his grandfather Devil Anse's knee, listening to exciting tales of hunting bears or tracking panthers through the deep woods near his home. Coleman loved the stories. And as he grew into adolescence, he still listened intently—often asking a lot of questions—as family members shared incidents relating to the feud. It was these accounts that stirred a passion in Coleman for history. By the time the above image was taken, the feud had been over for many years, and it was the time of the next generation to stand up and be counted. Coleman took careful aim at the future, deciding to head off to law school, while at the same time continuing his passion of studying feud history. Throughout the remainder of his life, Coleman authored lengthy journals and recorded audiotapes in an effort to preserve his grandfather's stories and document family events as a record of the Hatfield clan's history. His research concerning the Hatfield and McCoy feud is still being studied today. (Courtesy of the Coleman C. Hatfield collection.)

By the turn of the century, Devil Anse Hatfield was world-famous, as the violent story of the feud had been told and retold in newspapers and periodicals around the globe. In an illustration of reality meeting show business, this image of Anse was one of a peculiar series of publicity shots taken to promote an early silent movie. The short film, shot mostly in West Virginia, was intended to depict the history, drama, and action connected with the Hatfield and McCoy feud. Devil Anse signed on early to appear in the production, portraying himself in the lead role. The film's limited theatrical release was never deemed a box office success, likely because of issues related to funding its national distribution. Unfortunately for historians, no known copies of the film reels survived the decades. The *Logan Democrat* from October 9, 1913, reported that Devil Anse was considering opening a vaudeville show, but no further records pertaining to the show were published. (Courtesy of the Coleman C. Hatfield collection.)

Logan County sheriff Don Chafin (center) stands in front of the Logan County Courthouse in 1921 with his deputies and resident supporters. Chafin, a controversial figure sometimes called the "King of Logan County," had long been involved in local politics, previously having been the county's assessor. He was also a successful business owner and entrepreneur.

James "Slater Jim" Hatfield (left) was an uncle of Devil Anse. Because Slater Jim briefly deserted the Confederate army during the Civil War, an officer ordered Devil Anse to execute his uncle. Anse refused, and after a series of related occurrences, Slater Jim was allowed to live. Nevertheless, this episode prompted Anse to leave the army by the end of 1863. Jim is shown with Rachel Toler. (Courtesy of the Coleman C. Hatfield collection.)

In response to the mine wars and by order of Pres. Warren G. Harding, the first federal troops arrived at the communities of Jeffrey, Blair, Sharples, and Logan to reestablish order in the coalfields around Blair Mountain on September 3, 1921. Here, troops come by rail to the rear of Logan near the depot. When confronted with the likelihood of fighting against US troops, most of the protesting miners surrendered.

In August 1921, as many as 5,000 angry coal miners marched from Marmet toward Logan to protest deplorable work conditions in local coalfields. Logan County sheriff Don Chafin mobilized an opposing army to battle protesters and impede the march. Tensions grew and violence broke out between the factions at Blair Mountain, the natural barrier outside of Logan. By September, under presidential orders, federal troops arrived in Logan via train to restore order.

At the time of the Blair Mountain War, federal troops arrived in the city of Logan, and a local command post was set up inside the Aracoma Hotel, the structure shown at the right of this image. According to the West Virginia State Archives, Blair Mountain remains a powerful symbol for workers to this day.

In August 1921, the era of the Blair Mountain War prior to the arrival of federal troops, supporters of Sheriff Don Chafin's nonunion faction gathered at the Aracoma Hotel to prepare for combat against protesting miners marching toward Logan County. Chafin's volunteer militia was heavily armed with rifles, shotguns, tommy guns, nightsticks, and handguns. Machine gun nests in the courthouse were established, in case marchers ever entered the city. (Courtesy of Kenneth King.)

On the first Sunday after his election as sheriff in 1920, "Dapper Don" Chafin posed for this image outside his home on Main Street in Logan. County historian Robert Y. Spence once wrote that this photograph, made by the Bachrach Studio, is "an ideal likeness of Chafin in his heyday," adding that Chafin "looked capable, determined, and self-confident to the point of arrogance. He had all those traits. He was rough. And he was remarkably successful as he controlled county politics." During Don Chafin's reign as sheriff, Logan continually made state headlines due to his and his associates' unyielding style of leadership, which included partisan shenanigans, cronyism, corruption, intimidation, and brutal beatings. Soon after the election, Chafin also became heavily involved in labor relations in the county, especially as it concerned the mining industry. Because of his nonunion stance, Chafin's confrontations with union organizers and actions against employee organization led to a heating-up of labor tensions, setting the stage for the forthcoming Blair Mountain War in 1921.

In this 1959 image, US Senator Robert C. Byrd and his wife, Erma, meet with politicians Claude Ellis and Tom Godby (right) to discuss factional politics. Senator Byrd often campaigned in the county and visited the region on other occasions over the decades, cultivating many friendships along the way. Ellis, a lifelong resident of Logan County and a member of the Young Democrats in the late 1950s, led the John F. Kennedy for President campaign in the county in 1960. He worked closely with the Kennedys, especially with John, Robert, and Edward, and traveled with the family on the state campaign trail. During this period, he was considered a powerful county political boss. A Logan County deputy, he became a successful business owner and was eventually appointed to the Liquor Commission. Ellis later served as a justice of the peace. He was a city councilman and, in his later years, became a popular mayor of Logan. Tom Godby was also a noted individual in the county and a longtime politician. He served as Logan's county assessor for many years.

Poet Thomas Dunn English was born on June 29, 1819, in Pennsylvania. He resided in Logan County from 1852 to 1856. Before moving to Lawnsville (now the city of Logan) he worked as an editor in New York. Historian Robert Y. Spence once wrote that news of Logan's vast coal reserves and timber assets prompted English to move to the coalfields, where he bought multiple coal leases and incorporated two coal companies. English also got involved in local government. Lawnsville had never been incorporated until he and others petitioned the General Assembly of Virginia to incorporate the town as Aracoma. English served as the town's postmaster, and was later elected mayor. In 1856, when his coal speculations failed, English and his wife moved to Virginia. He is best known for his 1843 ballad "Ben Bolt." However, his Mountain State poems include "The Logan Grazier" and "Rafting on the Guyandotte." English later settled in New Jersey. In 1862, he was elected to one term in the New Jersey legislature, and later, he served two terms in Congress. He died on April 1, 1902.

One of the fathers of the county, Henry Clay Ragland, was a brilliant attorney, writer, politician, and pioneer newspaper publisher. The *Logan County Banner* began publication on March 7, 1889, with Ragland as editor. The newspaper published every Thursday from its offices at 412 Main Street. One of his first published editorials on April 25, 1889, called for the immediate construction of a railroad in Logan. This became a recurring theme in the publication over the years. County historian Robert Y. Spence described him as politically minded and opinionated, saying, "[Ragland was] a fiery Democrat and a dedicated populist of the type that fought for the agrarian protestors of the 1890s. He was a supporter of William Jennings Bryan, the Democrat furthest to the political left in that decade. When Bryan ran for president . . . Ragland dropped out of his own race for Logan County prosecutor so he could devote all his time to Bryan's campaign." He also wrote that Ragland was not a man to keep his mouth shut about much of anything.

Above, Claude Ellis owned the Smoke House Restaurant and was a powerful political leader at the time this image was taken in the late 1970s or early 1980s. Ellis owned a variety of business interests, including rental property and a filling station located at the intersection of Dingess and Water Streets. In 1960, he led the local John F. Kennedy for President campaign, and he helped manage county politics for many decades. In the image below, Claude Ellis stands with Franklin D. Roosevelt Jr. (center) and Raymond Chafin at the Logan County Courthouse at the height of the John F. Kennedy presidential primary campaign in 1960. Franklin D. Roosevelt Jr. was traveling through the state campaigning for Kennedy. Chafin, who was from Cow Creek, was the leader of the Hubert Humphrey for President campaign and faction at the time.

Chester Cush Chambers, better known as Judge C.C. Chambers, was born on December 18, 1890, near Pecks Mill. He served as county recorder, and he was the mayor and city attorney for Logan. He was eventually elected county circuit judge in 1936 and served through 1968, when he retired.

This all-star high school team—and future college and professional basketball greats—gathered at Williamson Fieldhouse in Mingo County around 1960 to face Kentucky. Number 14, Willie Akers, later became a West Virginia University (WVU) standout and a Logan High School coaching legend. Number 12 is WVU and NBA legend Jerry West. Number 7, George Ritchie, played at Wake Forest and coached at Williamson. Jay Jacobs, number 3, was a WVU player and radio commentator. (Courtesy of Kyle Lovern and George Ritchie.)

A city father who helped change the face of Logan County over his lifetime, Bruce McDonald was born at Huff Creek on February 8, 1860. He attended local schools, and after completion, he sought further education at Athens Old Concord Church, taught by Captain French in Mercer County. In the fall of 1885, McDonald entered National Normal University, at Lebanon, Ohio. Bruce ran as the Democratic candidate for the state legislature in 1904, was elected, and served through 1908. He was then nominated as a commissioner of the county court from 1912 to 1919, serving six years as president. He and his brother Millard were affiliated with a mercantile business at Huff Creek. Bruce eventually moved to Taplin and continued the mercantile business for the next 15 years. He was eventually vice president of the W.W. McDonald Land Company, the largest holding company in the valley; one of the organizers and the vice president of the Guyan Valley Bank; and a member of the board of directors of the First National Bank.

Henry D. Hatfield was arguably the most distinguished and influential of the Hatfield clan, having become a physician, member of the McDowell County Court, governor, and US senator. Henry was born on Mate Creek in present-day Mingo County, the son of a Confederate soldier and nephew of Devil Anse Hatfield. He graduated from Franklin College at age 15 and received his medical degree from the University of Louisville at age 19. In 1904, Hatfield received a second medical degree with a concentration in surgery from New York University. He worked as a railroad surgeon, mine physician, and Mingo County's health commissioner. After serving briefly on the McDowell County Court, he was elected to the state senate and was chosen as its president in 1911. He was elected as the 14th governor of West Virginia in 1912, the youngest at that time. In 1928, he reentered politics and ran for the US Senate. Winning against Matthew M. Neely, he served one term and returned to his medical practice afterward. (Courtesy of the Coleman C. Hatfield collection and the West Virginia Archives.)

Democratic presidential candidate Sen. John F. Kennedy visited Logan County on numerous occasions in 1960 while campaigning for the Democratic nomination for president. Here, Kennedy stands at the counter of the Smoke House Restaurant in downtown Logan. Restaurant owner Albert Klele Sr. and waitress Verla Runyon stand behind the register. Besides eating at the local restaurant, Kennedy and his brothers lodged at the Aracoma Hotel on several occasions.

From left to right, Claude Ellis, Robert F. Kennedy, John W. Davis Jr., Raamie Barker, and Lester "Bus" Perry pose outside the Logan County Courthouse shortly after Kennedy spoke to an enormous crowd of supporters in downtown Logan in 1968. At the time, Barker led the Robert F. Kennedy for President campaign in Logan County. (Courtesy of Raamie Barker.)

There is always excitement at the Logan County Courthouse at a swearing-in ceremony of newly elected politicians. This image was taken in 1952. The woman at left administering the oath is unidentified, but the local politicians appear from left to right as follows: Oscar Smith, Avril Hunter, Dr. H.H. Cudden, Sam Mureddu, Robert McCormick, Herb Gibson, unidentified, Mr. Waugh, and Litz McQuire. (Courtesy of Kenneth King.)

During his campaign in 1968, Robert F. Kennedy came to the city of Logan. Just like when his brother John F. Kennedy campaigned in 1960, the crowds were auspiciously supportive and clamored to get close to the candidate. This image was taken at the courthouse square. Numerous local and state politicians sat on the platform, including Ken Hechler, Tom Godby, Claude Ellis, and Raamie Barker. (Courtesy of Raamie Barker.)

Four

DISASTERS AND CHALLENGES

It was a time of overwhelming sadness. On February 26, 1972, one of the deadliest floods in US history took place in Buffalo Creek Hollow in Logan County. Pittston Coal Company's coal slurry impoundment dam No. 3 had burst. Within minutes, 125 were dead, 1,100 were injured, and 4,000 were homeless. Seven were never found. (Courtesy of Ken Scaggs and Sherri Scaggs Smith.)

This photograph, taken by county aviator Grady Yeager, was documented as one of the first airplane crashes to take place in Logan County. This biplane, piloted by Raymond Woody, crashed near Chapmanville on April 18, 1937. The first airport in the county was located near Chapmanville and was under the management of Harry W. Rupert. A second airstrip opened for business at Taplin in 1946.

After the devastating 1963 flood, most of downtown Logan and other parts of the county remained submerged under water. This image looking toward Wilson Cleaners and A&P Supermarket shows Triangle Addition near the entrance to the city. The cleanup process lasted for weeks after the water receded.

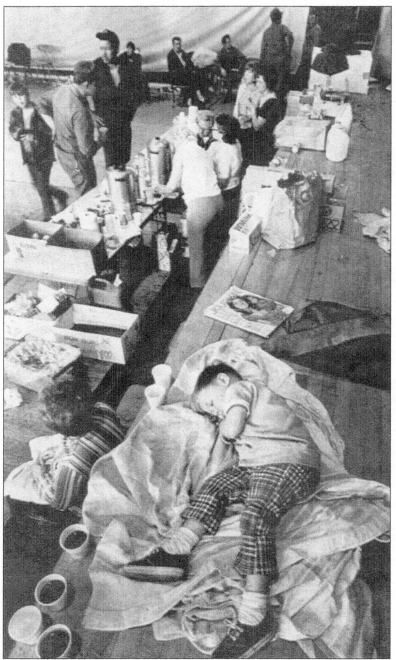

In 1972, a local newspaper reported that "life forever changed that day" for many families in Logan County's Triadelphia District. Immediately following the Buffalo Creek tragedy, most of the 4,000 individuals left homeless sought food, shelter, and assistance at the emergency command center set up at the Man Senior School gymnasium. Due to the results of a 30-foot wall of water and debris roaring through the hollow, 507 homes, 44 mobile homes, and 30 businesses were destroyed. The disaster destroyed or damaged homes in the communities of Amherstdale, Lundale, Saunders, Crites, Latrobe, Lorado, and others. The image comes from the *Logan News*. (Courtesy of Ken Scaggs and Sherri Scaggs Smith.)

On February 26, 1972, the Buffalo Creek flood disaster touched several communities and thousands of individuals, bringing death, destruction, and heartache to the region. This image was taken in the community of Becco after the Buffalo Creek dam burst. Homes, businesses, vehicles, and debris were piled high. (Courtesy of Ken Scaggs and Sherri Scaggs Smith.)

Charles T. Murphy, a local federal employee who was assisting flood survivors, photographed this image depicting the devastation several days after the Buffalo Creek disaster took place in February 1972. The sheer power behind the wall of moving water and sludge shoved steel bridges, homes, mobile homes, and wreckage up the hollow. (Courtesy of Charles T. Murphy.)

In this heartrending image taken in 1972 for the *Logan News*, hundreds of survivors gathered in Man, West Virginia, after the Buffalo Creek flood. Residents waited for assistance and for news of missing family members. Red Cross workers, National Guard troops, state and federal employees, and hundreds of volunteers came to Triadelphia District to help survivors of the flood and to continue an intensive search of the 22-mile hollow. According to the *Logan Banner*, an estimated 135 million gallons of water, sludge, and sticky mud backed up behind the dam area as up to four inches of rain fell in the 24 hours preceding the flood. The pressure and the stress were too great for the dam. The disaster remains one of the most lethal floods in US history. (Courtesy of Ken Scaggs and Sherri Scaggs Smith.)

This is another image taken of Buffalo Creek flood victims at the evacuation center in the gymnasium at Man High School. Local relief organizations moved quickly to assist survivors. Joe Patterson and Lila Hinchman of the Red Cross, Earl Jarvis of Logan County's PRIDE organization, and the Salvation Army were among the first responders. The Buffalo Mining Company also set up a claims office. (Courtesy of Ken Scaggs and Sherri Scaggs Smith.)

Astonishingly, steel railroad tracks were severed, twisted, and shoved from their ties, due to the sheer brute force of the rushing waters during the Buffalo Creek disaster on February 26, 1972. The pile of debris shown on the creek bank had once been a house that was instantly destroyed from the wall of floodwaters. (Courtesy of Charles T. Murphy.)

The above picture shows the power of the flood obliterating a mobile home. In the bottom image, cars, homes, and debris collide as the flood leaves miles of devastation. Historian Robert Y. Spence wrote about the disaster in his book *Land of the Guyandot*: "There had been warnings for years that the dam owned by the Pittston Coal Company was weak. In 1967, a heavy rain caused the dam to slip and the coal company had been warned . . . and the warnings were dismissed as the statements of alarmists. Then early in the morning of Saturday, February 26, 1972, the dam collapsed and roared down the valley, destroying 16 mining communities with 132 million gallons of water and one million tons of sludge, taking at least 125 lives." (Above, courtesy of Charles T. Murphy; below, courtesy of Ken Scaggs and Sherri Scaggs Smith.)

"It looked more like there had been a war there than a flood," said Carl Bradford, then working for West Virginia governor Arch A. Moore Jr. During the 1972 Buffalo Creek tragedy, the devastation seemed endless. The homes in the above image were picked up and thrown by the impact of the floodwaters. In the bottom image, West Virginia governor Arch Moore came to the flood site, spoke with emergency workers, and met with families. In 1972, Robert Y. Spence reported in an article in the *Logan News* that the governor—in the midst of a reelection bid—named a committee to investigate the matter. Named to the committee were J.H. Kelley, John Ashcraft, Ira Latimer, Elizabeth Hallanan, Charles D. Hylton, Julian F. Murrin, and representatives of the US Bureau of Mines and the US Geological Survey. (Courtesy of Charles T. Murphy.)

Barrels of clean drinking water were trucked into the community of Lorado for residents who had survived the Buffalo Creek disaster. Milk cartons and plastic jugs were provided for inhabitants, and food stations were set up in the community. An article in the *Logan News* from February 1972 described the circumstances: "The evacuation center at the Man Senior High School is a story of despair. Young and old wander throughout the school with dazed expressions, some of them in shock, some now realizing the full impact of the calamity that resulted when the dam broke at the head of Buffalo Hollow last Saturday morning." In the image at right, the community of Low Ash was also devastated from the flood. (Both, courtesy of Ken Scaggs and Sherri Scaggs Smith.)

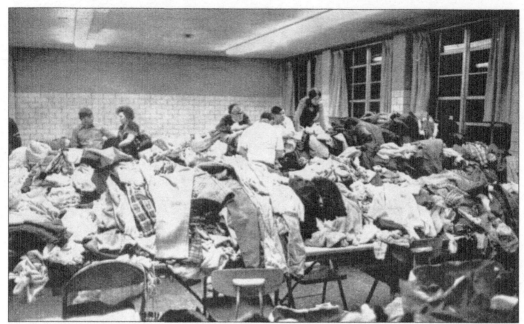

At the evacuation center at Logan High School following the Buffalo Creek flood, the regional Salvation Army and other relief organizations provided mounds of clothing and shoes for victims of the disaster. Also, drinking water, food, and other necessities for the flood survivors were made available. There was an outpouring of generosity from people from across the state and nation as clean up efforts began. (Courtesy of Ken Scaggs and Sherri Scaggs Smith.)

Unfortunately, there have been numerous train wrecks, derailments, and crashes in Logan County since the Chesapeake & Ohio Railroad first began construction on its rail system in the county in 1891. This image illustrates a catastrophic wreck at Dingess Run in June 1921. The *Logan County Banner* reported there was one fatality, tons of coal dumped along the rails, and several derailed train cars.

In 1963, after days of hard rain, the soil became saturated and flash flood waters elevated quickly and rushed over the Midelburg Addition Bridge. Tons of sludge and debris, swept up by the fury of the rushing water, accumulated at the crest of the bridge, and water levels continued to rise through the early afternoon. At the same time, waters raced into east-end residences and the business district of Logan.

Logan flood Jan. 28, 1918

The coalfields have always been susceptible to small stream and flash flooding, and the result is usually overwhelming destruction, heartache, and a long period of cleanup. In this image from January 1918, the city of Logan was once again flooded on the east end of town and in the central region. Major property damage was reported in the local newspaper.

The *Logan County Banner* of March 25, 1927, contained an article telling about Island Creek Coal Company's plan to create a community and a coal mine to be called Holden 22, which would soon be a major employer in the region. This photograph depicts the opening day of the mine and nearby coal camp, attended by several Island Creek Coal Company officials. In later years, the newspaper described the same mine as the site of "a dark chronicle of great loss for Logan County." It was here on March 8, 1960, that one of the worst mining accidents in county history took place. That day, 18 men perished—asphyxiated during a deadly blaze—in the deep mine. The fire is believed to have initially started when a slate fall snapped a high voltage trolley cable, which in turn ignited timbers supporting the roof. The event is still remembered locally as the Holden 22 Mine Disaster. The workers who perished collectively left behind 16 widows and 77 children.

Five

THROUGH THE YEARS

Through the years, the people of Logan County have been innovative and resourceful. A grinding mill and water wheel, likely constructed prior to the Civil War, existed near the community of Pecks Mill. Running water was abundant. For years, the prosperous enterprise, owned by the Peck family, ground wheat, corn, and other grains into flour. This image remains of the millstone from the county mill.

In this image, a young Coleman A. Hatfield proudly stands in a rowboat along the Tug River near War Eagle in present-day Mingo County. It was a location with historical significance relative to the feud. The period was approximately 1910. The grandson of Devil Anse Hatfield and son of Cap Hatfield, Coleman later studied law and became a practicing attorney in Logan County. Besides maintaining a flourishing law practice, he also had a lifelong passion for history and research, especially relating to the Hatfield family. He spent his adult life studying, researching, and verifying the Hatfield and McCoy feud. As an adult, he was considered the primary expert in West Virginia on Hatfield family history, having maintained extensive journals, manuscripts, and audiotaped interview materials on the subject. Throughout his career in Logan, Coleman was legally blind, though he never allowed the impairment to deter his varied interests.

DEMPSEY, HOUDINI, LEONARD

This undated publicity photograph shows heavyweight boxing champ Jack Dempsey throwing a punch at magician Harry Houdini (right) and Benny Leonard. Logan County historian G.T. Swain once wrote, "While it is true that William Harrison Dempsey, better known as Jack Dempsey, former heavyweight champion of the world, was born at Manassa, Colorado, June 24, 1895, he claims Logan as his native county, for it was here . . . he spent his boyhood years." Dempsey was the son of Hiram and Celia Smoot Dempsey, both born at Island Creek. In 1893, Hiram moved his family to Colorado, where Jack was born. When Jack was five, the Dempseys returned to Logan. When old enough to secure a job, he worked at a bowling alley in downtown Logan, and he eventually worked for Gay Coal & Coke Company, one mile west of Logan. Ultimately, due to a desire to prizefight, Dempsey caught a train and headed west to seek his fortune. From 1911 to 1916, he boxed in mining camps in Colorado, and by age 24, he had won 80 professional bouts. He went on to gain the heavyweight title in 1919. His nickname during this period was the "Manassa Mauler."

Still a common site in Logan County is car after car of bituminous coal being transported through the winding coalfields. These wooden cars are from the 1940s; however, trains and train cars much like this have been responsible for transporting "black gold" ever since locomotives first arrived at the cradle of the Appalachian Mountains.

Although the city of Logan was still an isolated region in 1910—with few roads and no utilities or infrastructure—the signs of new growth were taking hold. A second bank, Logan National Bank, had just opened in 1906, and the timber industry was bringing new jobs to the region. The coal boom was just launching, and mining companies were buying up large tracts of land in regions surrounding the county seat, including Holden and Island Creek.

Built by Island Creek Coal Company, the Whitman YMCA was a popular retreat for residents in the community when this image was made in 1921. Whitman, like other coal camps in the county, had an auditorium, a community church, rows of similar one-story homes, and other public buildings for the benefit of their employees. (Courtesy of Joe Hensley.)

Some things change, and some things remain the same. This picture was taken around 1921 by Carter's Studio, but Dingess Street has changed little over the last nine decades. The narrow street, sidewalks, and some original buildings still exist on the city street.

Railroad workers are pictured at the mammoth Peach Creek train yard in the 1930s. The yard—with its belching steam engines, numerous on-duty rail workers, roundhouse, yard office, and multilane tracks—was once one of Logan County's largest employers and a booming center of human activity. Freight and passenger trains traveling through the county nearly always passed through this facility, which featured a maze of tracks and locomotives. There were neighboring communities like Peach Creek, Crooked Creek, and West Logan, which provided housing for many of the railroad workers and their families. All were fast-growing communities at this point in Logan's history. And in earlier days before housing became more plentiful, wooden train cars were occasionally made available for new employees and their families. Heavy curtains could be hung in a particular car, separating it in half so that two families could live in a single car until they could find other living arrangements.

In this well-worn image, L. Harrison and his small road crew guide livestock teams, which are harnessed to heavy equipment, through the neighborhood. Working through the spring season, the road crew's project was to construct and level portions of Dingess Street in the city of Logan. This photograph was taken on May 27, 1909. (Courtesy of Ralph and Mildred Queen.)

During Prohibition, there were speakeasies in the county where immoral activities flourished and illegal alcoholic beverages were sold. For example, on the second floor of this building on Stratton Street (that now houses Super Dollar) was the location of a secret-key club called the Amour Club. Members were given entrance keys to the rooms where moonshine whiskey drinking, gambling, and romantic rendezvous took place.

This image from the 1920s is of the Craneco logging camp. The campsite offered semiprivate housing and bathhouses for its employees. Also, common areas and dining halls were provided. At this time, freshly cut beams were brought out of the woods by rail, though pack mules or workhorses were still used when logs were cut away from the train and had to be dragged long distances to the tracks.

Scott McDonald stands alongside young Arthur Justice in this image from the 1920s. McDonald had a farm at Crooked Creek but eventually sold the property to the railroad when it first came into the county, purchasing a smaller tract to farm nearby. Scott, like others during the period, had a love for the land and an appreciation for the quiet tranquility that comes with living in the countryside.

126

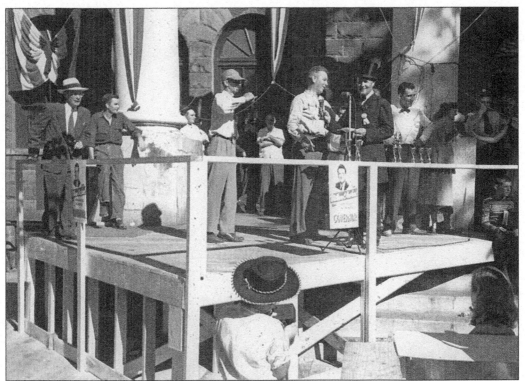

The City of Logan Centennial was held from Wednesday, September 10, through Saturday, September 13, 1952, and included a full program of events. Mayor McGuire, in the top hat, introduced a number of dignitaries on Saturday from a wooden platform in front of the courthouse. Later that evening, a square dance featuring Richard Cox and the Harvesters from WSAZ-TV was held. Earlier in the week, a mock parade was held on Stratton Street; residents dressed up in a variety of costumes, including the "Robbie the Robot" getup below. Other events included a raccoon hunt, a wood-chopping and coal-loading tournament, an old-timer's reunion, a mine rescue demonstration, beauty pageants, and an air show presented by the Air National Guard. A special production of *The Aracoma Story*, an outdoor drama, was also held at Midelburg Island.

Visit us at
arcadiapublishing.com

9 781531 654733